To
"The Adventurers"

Wild Thing (Harry),

Butler (Naomi),

Peanut (Beth), and

Krispy (Krissy)

— for the wild adventures
we've had and the ones we've
yet to encounter…

And to Helen — my warmest thanks.

This collection copyright © 1999 by Simon James

Text copyright © year of publication by individual authors
as noted in Acknowledgments

Illustrations copyright © 1999 by Simon James

First U.S. edition 2000

Library of Congress Cataloging-in-Publication Data
Days like this : a collection of small poems / selected and illustrated by Simon James
p.   cm.
Summary: A collection of short poems by such authors as Eve Merriam,
Ogden Nash, and Charlotte Zolotow.
ISBN 0-7636-0812-2
1. Children's poetry, American.   [1. American poetry—Collections.]
I. James, Simon, date.
PS586.3.D39   1999
811.008'09282—dc21   99-11363

2 4 6 8 10 9 7 5 3

Printed in Hong Kong

This book was typeset in Garamond ITC Book Condensed.
The illustrations were done in pen and ink and watercolor.

Candlewick Press
2067 Massachusetts Avenue
Cambridge, Massachusetts 02140

Days Like This

a collection of small poems
selected and illustrated by

Simon James

CANDLEWICK PRESS
CAMBRIDGE, MASSACHUSETTS

The Adventurers

We love adventures,
Where we live is
anybody's guess.

We love the open land
and the open land
is our address.

Simon James

Stepping Stones

Stepping over stepping stones, one, two, three,
Stepping over stepping stones, come with me.
The river's very fast,
And the river's very wide,
And we'll step across on stepping stones
And reach the other side.

Traditional

A Lazy Thought

There go the grownups
To the office,
To the store.
Subway rush,
Traffic crush;
Hurry, scurry,
Worry, flurry.

No wonder
Grownups
Don't grow up
Any more.

It takes a lot
Of slow
To grow.

Eve Merriam

The Guppy

Whales have calves,
Cats have kittens,
Bears have cubs,
Bats have bittens;
Swans have cygnets,
Seals have puppies,
But guppies just have
little guppies.

Ogden Nash

Sledding

Look at us
As we go
Sledding on the bright white snow.

Faces beaming
Long hair streaming
Passing those who are too slow.

Wendy Elizabeth Johnson

On My Little Guitar

On my little guitar
With only one string
I play in the moonlight
Any old thing.

C. Louis Leipoldt

Rain

Rain on the green grass,
And rain on the tree,
And rain on the housetop,
But not upon me.

Traditional

Tomorrow

Tomorrow's never there.
It always runs away.
Every time I catch it
It says it's called Today.

Steve Turner

The Picnic

We brought a rug for sitting on,
Our lunch was in a box.
The sand was warm. We didn't wear
Hats or Shoes or Socks.

Waves came curling up the beach.
We waded. It was fun.
Our sandwiches were different kinds.
I dropped my jelly one.

Dorothy Aldis

The Wind Came Running

The Wind came running
over the sand,
it caught and held me
by the hand.

It curled and whirled
and danced with me
down to the edge
of the dashing sea.

We danced together,
the Wind and I,
to the cry of a gull
and a wild sea cry.

Ivy O. Eastwick

25

First Day at School

My first day at school to-day.
Funny sort of day.
Didn't seem to learn much.
Seemed all we did was play.

Then teacher wrote some letters
On a board all painted black,
And then we had a story and ...
I don't think I'll go back.

Rod Hull

Sleeping Outdoors

Under the dark
is a star,
Under the star
is a tree,
Under the tree
is a blanket,
And under the blanket
is me.

Marchette Chute

The Summer Sun

Yes,
The sun shines bright
In the summer,
And the breeze is soft
As a sigh.

Yes,
The days are long
In the summer,
And the sun is king
Of the sky.

Wes Magee

The Seed

How does it know,
this little seed,
if it is to grow
to a flower or weed,

if it is to be
a vine or shoot,
or grow to a tree
with a long deep root?

A seed is so small
where do you suppose
it stores up all
of the things it knows?

Aileen Fisher

Bouncing

My mom,
bounce,
doesn't like it.
My dad,
bounce,
goes out of his head.
But I love to bounce,
bounce, bounce
on top of my bed.

My mom,
bounce,
calls out.
My dad,
bounce,
shouts from the hall.
But when I'm bouncing,
bouncing, bouncing,
I take no
bounce
notice at all.

Simon James   35

Pink Azalea

I feel as though
this bush were grown
especially for me.

I feel as though
I almost am
this little flowering tree.

Charlotte Zolotow

Two in Bed

When my brother Tommy
Sleeps in bed with me
He doubles up
And makes
himself
exactly
like
a
V
And 'cause the bed is not so wide
A part of him is on my side.

Abram Bunn Ross

My Love For You

I know you little,
I love you lots;
My love for you
Would fill ten pots,
Fifteen buckets,
Sixteen cans,
Three teacups,
And four dishpans.

Traditional

Today

Yesterday has gone
Tomorrow's yet to be,
Today is now
and always here
For everyone to see.

Simon James

Index of Titles

ACKNOWLEDGMENTS

The publisher would like to thank the copyright holders for permission to reproduce the following: **"First Day at School"** from *The Reluctant Pote*. Copyright © 1983 by Rod Hull. Reprinted by permission of Hodder and Stoughton Limited. **"The Guppy"** from *Verses From 1929 On* by Ogden Nash. Copyright © 1944 by Ogden Nash. First appeared in *The Saturday Evening Post*. Reprinted by permission of Little, Brown and Company. **"A Lazy Thought"** from *There Is No Rhyme for Silver* by Eve Merriam. Copyright © 1962 by Eve Merriam, copyright © renewed 1990 by Eve Merriam. Reprinted by permission of Marian Reiner. **"On My Little Guitar"** by C. Louis Leipoldt, translated by A. Delius. Reprinted by kind permission of Dr. Peter Shields. **"The Picnic"** from *Hop, Skip and Jump!* by Dorothy Aldis. Copyright © 1934 by Dorothy Aldis, copyright © renewed 1961 by Dorothy Aldis. Reprinted by permission of G.P. Putnam's Sons, a division of Penguin Putnam Inc. **"Pink Azalea"** from *River Winding*. Copyright © 1970 by Charlotte Zolotow. Reprinted by permission of S©ott Treimel New York for the author. **"The Seed"** from *Up the Windy Hill* by Aileen Fisher. Copyright © 1953 by Aileen Fisher, copyright © renewed 1981 by Aileen Fisher. Reprinted by permission of Marian Reiner for the author. **"Sleeping Outdoors"** from *Rhymes About Us* by Marchette Chute. Published 1974 by E.P. Dutton. Copyright © 1974 by Marchette Chute. Reprinted by permission of Elizabeth Roach. **"The Summer Sun"** by Wes Magee, from *Dragon Smoke: Poetry One*. Published 1985 by Basil Blackwell. Copyright © 1985 by Wes Magee. Reprinted by permission of the author. **"Tomorrow"** from *The Day I Fell Down the Toilet and Other Poems*. Published 1996 by Lion Books. Copyright © 1996 by Steve Turner. Reprinted by kind permission of the author and Lisa Eveleigh. **"The Wind Came Running"** by Ivy O. Eastwick from *Cherry Stones! Garden Swings!* by Ivy O. Eastwick. Copyright © 1962 by Abingdon Press. Reprinted by permission of the publisher. **"The Adventurers," "Bouncing,"** and **"Today"** are copyright © 1999 by Simon James. Every effort has been made to obtain permission to reprint copyright material, but there may be cases where we have been unable to trace a copyright holder. The publisher will be happy to correct any omission in future printings.